The how to guide for styling wedding & events

Introduction:

Module 1 Niche & your ideal client

Module 2 Research

Module 3 Colours & mood boards

Module 4 Resources

Module 5 Demo set up

Module 6 Setting up techniques

Module 7 Being creative

Module 8 Backdrops

Module 9 The admin side

Module 10 After set up & reviews

Module 1 Niche your ideal client

Objectives

- Have a better understanding of the term niche
- Be able to identify your ideal client

Introduction:

A first big factor when setting up any business, is working out your ideal client who is your business aimed at?

This then enables you to NICHE and really focus on attracting your audience, it is about bringing the right audience to you!

1.1

Niching is always very important! Once you know who your ideal client is, you can niche away and focus on that audience. This does not mean you will get less work, in fact when you niche you are opening the door so much more! You are attracting the audience right for your business.

Your ideal client is looking for a particular style or trend, so once they come across your work, you will more than likely be the one they use, as they are confident you can deliver exactly what they want!

The term NICHE – A denoting or relating to products, services or interests that appeal to a small, or specialised section of the population.

Taken from the dictionary

In my words – appealing to selected people of your CHOICE!

I want you to think about your business!

What do you want it to be like?

Look like?

What style do you want to deliver?

What trends do you want to use?

What do you see your future business looking like?

Once you have made your list this should help you think about your NICHE in more detail & have a better understanding of the meaning!

1.2

Identifying your ideal client is the next step, you should now have an understanding of NICHE and what you see your business looking like?

So let's identify your ideal client! Look at your answers from the previous task, does this give you any idea who your ideal client is?

Let's start this task and see if it helps you further!

Who is your client?

Age?

Style?

Budget type?

Want something different? Want what everyone else has?

Looking for budget décor?

Once you have answered these questions look at everything you have and write your NICHE & ideal client down, remember this is not a wrong or right answer, it is just for you, and it helps you narrow down your audience and advertise to your ideal client.

We don't all have the same which is why you are not shutting work down from others, as there is always jobs from clients you are attracting!! Making it no competition for anybody.

So giving you an example this is mine:

I am a massive PINTEREST fan, I get all my inspiration mainly from PINTEREST, so it was easier for me to narrow it right down, I love more stylish décor, eye catching, luxury & different, so I want to attract people just like me…. I want the PINTEREST bride the PINTEREST customers for events that is my ideal client a PINTEREST fan just like me!

Summary:

NICHE - appealing to your target audience, who are you?? What does your company stand for???

Work out your ideal client so you are constantly working on attracting the clients you want!

Your notes

Module 2: Researching the latest trends

Objectives:

- The importance of keeping up with the latest trends & new styles constantly
- To identify places to research for the latest trends

Introduction:

So the wedding & event industry changes styles constantly!!!!! Something that can be in demand can stay, while others can be a phase that only stick around for a short time! Until something new and stylish comes along!

Another thing to remember is budget when it comes to the latest trends!! Once something becomes in demand…. So does the cost…. So a high end client may go for something more popular and stylish then someone with a smaller budget. So it is important to work out what trends sit with what budget! The reason for this is not that someone on a budget can't have the latest, it is so you as the stylist can come up with something just as fantastic!

Let me give you an example of this…

A backdrop with nets, covered in a range of florals, high end client, you could go completely ott, lower budget, still use nets, but a less popular flower and more foliage, so the final look will be, a beautiful backdrop with different styles! So the trend & style is still there for both clients, just different! Which is what we want.

Research does really help with this! And it is important to be consistent with the research, you should be looking around at least once a month minimum, at the latest trends & styles.

1.1

It is so important to keep up with new trends & styles, firstly people want style, they want new, they want what everyone else has and they want eye catching décor.

Following all the newest trends & styles will attract customers, let's take a minute and think...

1. We have a trend that was popular back in 2015 let's say (a basic topiary tree)

And then we have

2. A big 2018 trend.. Blossom trees both small and large sized!

Both very similar in price!!

Which one would you rather!! So it is more about what the trend is other then what you like!

When you keep up with all the latest trends & styles it can lead to more work, good word of mouth getting your company talked about which is what we all want. Possibilities to be blogged and a longer running of your business.

Another important factor is it helps niche your clients, which we will cover more about. So you only need to research the type of trends & styles suitable to your niche.

2.1

So where can we research places to look??

The biggest growing platform for décor is PINTEREST!!! If you are not registered, please make sure this is the first thing you go ahead and do right now!!!!

It is amazing, people from all over the world share pictures, ideas, tips, templates & instructions, giving you complete inspiration to go away and put your own stuff together! Which I recommend, always put your twist to it, make it your own! That in itself will make you stand out from the rest!

Screenshot, make your own boards & pins, you can set up a personal & a business account, so you are keeping your inspiration pins separate to your work, and go ahead, get searching, you won't put your phone down for hours!!

There are so many bloggers, here is some of the best, look them up, look at the styles if you feel inspired give them a follow! Here are a few

- Rock My Wedding
- Before The Big Day
- Love My Dress
- Boho Weddings
- Bespoke Bride

- Whimsical Wonderland Weddings
- Brides Up North
- B.Loved
- Rock n Roll Bride
- English Wedding Blog

Do some adding on social media mainly Instagram, in the search bar type some key words, so example 'Blushweddings' it will show up something like 7000+ post, do some scrolling as you will find bloggers or professionals in the industry not on PINTEREST, so it will be more inspiration for you!

When adding remember to include some of the biggest names in the wedding industry such as, Hitched & The National Wedding Show, that will also help you stay in the loop!

Lastly have a little browse on ETSY, this is more of a shop for crafts, but it does give inspiration as a lot of items are handmade, sits well within wedding & events décor.

Summary:

Importance of keeping up with the latest trends will secure more bookings, people talking about your company, standing out & having a successful lengthy business!

Places to research all the latest trends

- Pinterest
- Wedding bloggers
- Instagram
- ETSY

Your notes:

Module 3: Colours & Mood boards

Objectives:

- Importance of colours
- Matching colours
- Where to find the latest colour trends
- How to create a mood board
- Benefits of mood boards for both you and clients

Introduction:

Colours colours colours…… Do they change?? Yes absolutely! You will always get a few popular colours that will always be around, however, you will find colours come and go.

Again back to your ideal client this can come into play, as colour choices can suit particular people and budgets.

Putting mood boards together is such a good idea! Not only for clients but for you to have a play around with, giving you some idea what colours work well together and also what may not! We have all been there when we get a little carried away! That is why mood boards can really help, so we don't get in the zone where it is too late, we have stock that just does not go!

1.1 1.2

When it comes to weddings & events it is really important to know about colours! What works well together & what trends are going off within the season!

Seasons can change the colour dramatically in weddings, what is popular & trending in the summer could be completely different in winter seasons!

A bride or someone hosting an event, want to believe the stylist knows what works well! A lot of people mainly brides are not always sure on what colours they want, they may have an idea, for example they say 'I want pink' ok and have you thought about another colour? 'No, what do you think?'

So you come into place with your advice & ideas, so now have a think what goes with pink? Match pink to both a summer season & winter, as they both can be completely different?

A little tip collect paint colour sample booklets from DIY shops, this will be easier to pair up colours, gives you the opportunity to visually see it in person!

1.3

So where can you go for all the latest trends???

Pinterest is so helpful, it is a big platform for the wedding & events industry, and it is constantly being updated with all the latest trends worldwide!

Instagram is another massive platform for the wedding & event industry, everyone loves an Instagram picture so here is where you will find some of the best work out there!

One thing I have also learned colours & trends follow through from the catwalk, if something is high on the catwalk it tends to follow through to most things! So yes it does follow through to the wedding industry!

Tip – The yearly pantone colour also plays a big part! Keep an eye out for the yearly colour. You can find this information on most search engines! Have ago now and make a note of this year's pantone colour! Now you know have you seen this colour around? Is it trending right now??

Also following wedding bloggers, professionals in the area or academies within the wedding and event industry will also inspire you and keep you on the latest trends!

Research top bloggers in the wedding industry, take a look at their website & social media platforms, make a list on each one, use the top 10, on what you like about them? Does their trend & style suit you? (Remember your niche here) could they help you to be inspired? Keep on trend? Once you have your notes, have a look over and select at least 5 to follow (You can do all if you choose) take a browse of their profile monthly keeping on top of the latest blogging posts!

Wedding academies are also another fantastic opportunity to keep up with the latest colour trends! For example I follow wedding academies and got a sneak peek at The International Wedding report for this year!! Was fantastic, here we got to look at the colour trends for the upcoming year! So defo a recommend for you to follow! Have a research and get adding on your social media!

2.1

So how can you create your own mood boards?? Download an app on your smart phone, the one I use is Layout. Browse any platforms, websites, Google or online magazines, screenshot the pictures that appeal to you, or what you are looking to use for a finished design. On your Layout app or whichever one is suitable to you, add your pictures and you will it lays them out like a mood board! Which is so helpful when you want to create a number of these for brides on a regular basis.

2.2

So what benefits do creating mood boards bring??? To be able to visualise your ideas for both you and your client!!

These really do bring your ideas to life, it makes it easier for both you and your clients to see what it could possibly look like all brought together. It's not like you can always set up to show your clients what their wedding/event could look like. They will not see till maybe the day! So putting together mood boards helps your client to see were you are coming from with all your ideas, also can clear up any confusion that sometimes can arise, if items are not shown previously!

Tip Do everything to always protect yourself, if you have done everything the right way, nothing can knock you!

Create a poll on your FB, do you use mood boards when designing your event?? Collect your information and see what your clients say!!

Notes:

Module 4: Finding resources

Objectives:

- Resources to think about
- Where to look for resources
- Using other companies

Introduction:

So when I say resources what do I mean?? So in some cases, you need to put together some demos, this is to showcase your work! What can you do? Create or make? People want to see, they want pictures, and they want visualisation! So resources it what you need to put into a demo, think of everything, items, people, venue & time!

1.1

So think about what you want to showcase, for example the last demos I completed were full table set ups in different styles & colours, to show what I am capable of putting together and helping my niche decide if I am the right company for them!

We will use a backdrop for an example! What resources do you need to create and showcase a backdrop?? Think of equipment & materials? Where will you set your backdrop up for pictures? Remember this is an important part (pictures in the front room are not a great showcase, unless you can use a complete blank wall, I will provide more information on this in a separate module) what is the costing for a venue? If you hire one?

Do you need anyone to help set up your backdrop up or is it a person set up frame? Will you be hiring a professional photographer to help you with pictures? How much time will you put into your day? Will you require any other resources?

Now resources is used for every décor set up you put together. You require resources for demos or on the day set ups! Another example, resource some table décor, put together your own little set ups for a place setting.

Activity – You are planning to create an aisle set up demo, start from the top and work out all your resources, what equipment do you need? Remember even the smallest things from scissors to pins! Where will your demo be located? When? Costings? And any help needed? Now put this into place and create your first demo!!

1.2 2.1

So where can you go to get your resources? Think about if it is a resource you will keep? So will it be something popular to hire out or worth your costing? Or can you source from another supplier for the day?

There are a few wedding décor companies online to search, a few of them are Wedding Mall & Wedding Mart give them a browse!

If you are looking to receive goods from China or other countries to import, Alibaba are very good for the wedding industry or Aliexpress!

You will also get approached on your social media by companies, always say thank you and have a browse, as you never know, some items can also be really unique! Just check them out before you commit to buying anything!

Ebay is also a very good one to browse on or Amazon, especially if you are looking to make things yourself, you can get some good craft materials from any of these websites!

Also sourcing from other suppliers, this is really good as it builds relationships. You don't always need to buy in everything yourself especially if it a big costing to purchase the first time, and you can't guarantee it will be hired out much after, then I recommend sourcing it!

So either join a FB group, or email a few local companies, so you are saving on mileage costings, and agree a fee to hire from them! However very important, be very clear!!! You don't want the company claiming the work, when all they did is supply, so just put it in writing what you want!

For example, Hi there I have a customer looking for 2 blossom trees, is this something I can hire from you for the day, and use within my portfolio of the set up?? Then from day dot you have been clear on what you want!! Avoid confusion and upset straight away!

When you source from other companies, you then build a relationship, were when they need something they do not have, were will they look first??? You!!!

Tasks – take a look at all the websites I provided you with, just have a browse see what you can find!

Find local suppliers to follow on social media that are similar to your niche, either introduce yourself first or find out if it is something they do, or just stay connected for now!

Notes:

Module 5: Demo set ups

Objectives:

- Planning demo set ups
- Why they are important
- The benefits of doing a demo set up

Introduction:

Now this is the fun part……. Get creative it's time to work on a demo!!! I believe demo set ups are so important!!! It is easy to say we can offer you a backdrop with the works, or we can offer you a centrepiece full of the season trends!! But where is the proof to that? Would you pay over £200 for centrepieces you had never seen, I don't mean necessarily the pacific design they want, but at least examples of what you can do, to show them you're trusting and capable! That is why a demo is important, gives the customer that guarantee you are capable, trustworthy & good at your job! You can show of your skills, be proud of what you do, show a way something can work, or let your clients visualise their way!!

1.1

So in the last module a task was to look into resources you will need, now put it into action!! So a demo does take a lot of planning as you need to think even about the costs, is the demo something that you are on a budget for as you just want to give some content to your audience? Or do you have a good budget to put towards it? Firstly plan your budget and what you plan on doing a demo for! Then go onto look into all your resources, sort your venue, again this can be at home if your background area is clear of all furniture and against a blank background! Bring in anyone you need to, & lastly put your stuff together and create a demo perfect for you and your company!

Your task is to do your demo!! Would love to see this so do feel free to send in your pictures to me, I will be sure to reply! Sarah@sparklingeventhire.com

2.1 2.2

So the importance and the benefits, I have already touched a little on the importance, I can't express enough how a good demo is important, sometimes before we get the customers we want and the profit, we need to show what you can do!

I always look at it as, would I pay let's say £1500 to £2000 for a full décor package, if I hadn't seen any of the companies work or know if they are right for me! The answer for me is NO!

So showcase even little, if I want to show of a new charger plate, I would clear an area, use a napkin that goes perfectly, create a design, add a name tag & some foliage and there you have it, a demo, showing what you can do!

Give it ago even small, set up a place setting at home, just clear the background and focus a picture just on the setting! Upload your design and let your niche clients see what you can do!

It gets people talking also, a demo you can create something to a style either you like, think is trending or just trying new things together! Upload it and friends, family & clients can get sharing, like what you do and bring you the visibility you need!

So your tasks are to put together at least 3 demos, can be small or big!! Get excited, as this is the fun parts!! I love them!! Do send pictures in, would love to see them!!!

Notes:

Module 6 Setting up techniques

Objectives

- How to prepare for set up
- Things to think about when setting up
- What to look out for
- Extra set up tips

Introduction:

So you are off to set up!!!!! How exciting!! Love this part, as much as it is nerve racking, as anything can happen!! But at the same time, all that planning, it is time to put it together!! The feeling you have after is just like wow I did this, I put this together!! Don't let the nerves get you, it is natural to feel like it and a good thing!! Shows you care, have passion and want everything to go well!!

So let's help!!

1.1

So can you prepare?? Firstly make sure you have everything you need, plan this the night before, giving plenty of time! If you can pack it in the car/van so all you have to do in the morning is go!! No panicking knowing everything is together, ready to go!

Send a message just a couple of days before the event, to the client, confirming everything on your invoice and discussed between you both, if anything crops up, you have time to sort anything out! This also gives the client a little reassurance that everything is under control and you will there when you said!

So I always plan for what ifs…….. Something may break and I need to stick it back, I may need to hang something, I may need extra for possible rips, I forgot one so I am short!! Many things can happen so this is why prepare!

Take spares of everything, I always take at least 5 spares, if I am doing chair covers & sashes!

Little task – I am your client, I want you to fit 20 chair covers & sashes, and I also requested a large 4ft floral heart to hang behind my top table! Now prepare your set up, what do you need?

2.1

So there is a few things to think about on a setup, firstly is making sure you have spoken to the venue previously, you have arranged the times you can access, when the clients will arrive and any requirements you need to set up! TIP if you need to access the venue earlier please do say, if your entire set up is going to take you between 3-4 hours, and you can't access till 10 and the client arrives at 1, I would ask to access at 8, we are all there to give the client what they have paid for and want, so the chances are the venue will be very accommodating!

So timings do work out your timings, add a little extra on top, for unloading or possible setbacks, sometimes, which I have found wedding coordinators or managers, end up wanting a chat! So that can take some tome away as well! Demos come in well for this as it gives you a little idea on time!

Do you need help!!! Extra hands family, friends or colleagues, if it is a complete set up that will take 3 hours alone, could you cut this down if you added an extra pair of hands!

Parking, is there parking, if not find your nearest and is there a time limit on unloading!

Next communicate about collection, both with your client and venue, so no confusion about where the items will be going, as you don't want things going missing! For weddings I tend to collect next day, so items are used through the entire day, smaller events find out when they finish and collect!

2.2

Things to look out for, firstly do your research into the venue, look at pictures get an idea on what you're working with! Check there is enough chairs, tables and any other furniture needed out ready, if a bride has paid for 100 chair sashes, make sure 100 are out, sometimes venues don't always put the correct out, or if they have had a lot cancelled! What I do in this situation, if a bride has paid 100 and 20 dropped out, I would ask for 10 extra, just to be dressed and jotted around as extra chairs for the evening, even if they are put away until later on, this way you have shown to the bride you stick by your agreement!

If you are doing any hanging on ceilings or walls, make sure you have all the equipment and resources to do so, and think about crop ups, this can happen! What are the walls can they be stuck too, hang on, worth fining this out before, but if that is not possible, then prepare yourself!

In case you was to forget anything, think about who is around on your event set up day just in case, can you get things dropped down to you or is there any shops near you! Always worth a look into!

Task – if you already have an event set up, make a list or just research into things that need to be looked out for and make a list to prepare yourself!

3.1

Extra tips, so check measurements for things, especially distance from ceiling or beams to the floor if you need to hang or drape, is it accessible? Can you do it? Would you need assistant? Measurements are so important!!!

Backdrop hired out, where is it going? Can it fit? Is the surface flat for the stand? If they require outside, check weather? Arrange an alternative just in case!

Always carry a glue gun, safety pins, pins and clips!!!! Massive tip!!!!!

Notes:

Module 7 Being creative & DIYING your events

Objectives

- Things to do yourself
- Getting creative
- Advertising your DIYS
- Offering DIY tips to customers

Introduction:

In the wedding and events industry, it is the best trade to get creative, to work in this industry you need to have that creative eye! Making something and seeing the finish! That is what we do with a wedding and an event, we start with a blank canvass and finish with a picture!

So why not add some DIY into events and get creative, there is so many little things you can get creative with!

1.1

So what type of things can you do yourself? I started with foliage & flower arranging, this doesn't even need to be real, you can use artificial! Go around your garden or have walk around the park, can you see some nice foliage you can play with? You can bring in spray paint to add glitter or change colours, give metallic ago, add some twine ribbon and see what you can come up with!

This would sit perfectly on a napkin, charger plate or under a nametag. Then go ahead and do a flower arrangement, if you would rather artificial, take a look around some home shops, collect a few to make a little arrangement, again this could sit within a chair sash or as an arrangement on the table!

Then try a few bigger tasks, have ago with some table stationary, try to create a menu, table number or nametags, you must remember copy rights! We are in an industry where our work stays close to heart, so using other people's work could damage your reputation, so do keep in mind when it comes to your designs! But who wants to copy? Defo no one here! So get down to some fun stuff and create something amazing!

Favours is another, have ago creating your own, so many favours you can get creative with, either work with a client's theme or just put a couple of designs together, one I made which was fun and unique, I made a flavoured for sugar for tea lovers, put it in a cute bottle and done a little foliage arrangement to go with it!

Events now again this is really fun especially parties as we can get even more creative and do so much! Try doing a party bag, a prop I love these!!! Thank you tags, party bag toys, or a backdrop, it can be so fun!

Again have a look through Pinterest for inspiration, or think of a baby shower, what personal touch could you add? Something different, could be a prop for tables or backdrop props!

So let's get creative!!!! Your task is to create a prop for a party, it is a baby boys 1st birthday party, make a suitable prop for pictures, the baby will next to your prop as a main feature, thin of cake smashing, a great picture with a main feature! Have fun!!!

2.1.

Getting creative is so much fun, it's relaxing and gives you something to get excited about when you think of a project! My newest creative project is calligraphy, this comes in play brilliant with the wedding industry, perfect for stationary! And fun for me!!

You can get creative in so many ways, one thing I also do, when I am at a wedding or event, if I have extra décor items, or taken a few things I thought myself would suit the theme, not necessarily in with the quote, but if you think it will look good, and does not put you out of pocket include it, it reflects you, and it would be appreciated, add it and get creative! I have done this many times, for an Alice in Wonderland theme I done, I added a large paper flower that was not included, but it didn't cost much to make and I knew it would look good!

So get creative with everything, this can also come into play when a client has a theme, but not yet a design or idea how to put there theme across, this is so much fun, you can design it yourself, use your imagination and your creativeness to really put together an amazing design, send pictures or even draw it to show your client!

So let's pan an event full of creativeness, we will continue with the baby boys 1st birthday party, you have created a prop, now let's make some favours, just do a sample, research, and have a think about what ideas you can do! Now do some little thank you tags to go with the favours, let's finish it with a table centrepiece, with more events again this can be more DIY, with a creative twist!

Have fun with this task!!

3.1

This is so important, get out there what you can do, how creative you can be, how unique, what information you need to come up with something amazing!

From stationary to favours, props & foliage arrangements, get them advertised, put them up on social media platforms, do an explanation, say how you made them, what you did if you like, and even create a little shop for your makes!

I made some unicorn wands from scratch, using my sewing machine, I put these up on my shop and advertised what I done, I get a really good response from it and feedback, gives you a little boost and gets people talking about just what you can do!

So once you have done a little make take some pictures, remember background keep it clear try and use a blank wall!

4.1

This is fun why not do some demonstrations, videos, lives or talks on some of your DIYS, this can really attract customers as your sharing some tips, yes it means some people can go of an do it themselves, but also it shows others who don't have that time, or that may not even be a little creative, just how good what you do is, they can personally see you do something, which gives trust and makes them think, I would love them to work for me!

I did a video on foliage arrangements, to go on the back of a lace chair hood, people loved it!! I got some more likes from it, I uploaded to some FB wedding groups, which got a lot of attention! So these benefit us, plus people can see a person behind the business, this can also help!

Give it ago and see some benefits, create a video, share it to your platforms and to some groups and see your audience grow, also a top tip, if you do this on a regular basis maybe once a month, it could really attract a fan base, which is a good way at getting visible!

So task is to put together a video of you making something, can be anything, were you are giving detail on the how too, share it and let your audience grow!!

Notes:

Module 8 Backdrops

Objectives

- Things to think about first when making a backdrop
- Putting designs together for a backdrop
- Backdrop frames
- Decorating your backdrop

Introduction:

So the market for backdrops is taking storm!!! Who does not want to walk down and stand in front of a beautiful setting while talking their vows, or sit in front of one at their wedding breakfast and have beautiful background pictures? Type wedding backdrop into Pinterest or party backdrop and be completely wowed, you will find so many beautiful designs!!

So get involved, you can create a backdrop just as beautiful, unique & wow someone else!!

1.1

So what resources do you need to create and showcase a backdrop?? First thing how are you going to create a backdrop? Do you require a stand & where will you purchase one from? Are you going to create a draped backdrop, curtain, flower, foliage, board or vinyl backdrop picture? How will it attach to the stand? What décor will you add? For example a curtain backdrop, I always include some flowers & foliage or will you add props? So much to think about when it comes to a backdrop!

So answer these questions first so it helps you come up with an idea on what you will work towards first!

2.1

So once you have done the first part this should give you an idea on what you want to work towards?

I will use an example I want to put together a white curtain net backdrop, pulled back with florals & foliage! So first thing I need to think about is the material, so I want white, but needs to be the correct style and sit correctly on the stand, best thing to do is research, look into different fabrics, other backdrops to see what the fabric is used, get an idea how this is going to hang the entire day securely while looking immaculate! Once you have an idea on fabric, it is time to style with flowers or foliage, what colours are you going for? And style? Will it be at the sides on the top or both?

Next with your design you need to think about how your attaching the flowers or foliage, will it be permeant or will you make it so you can use the backdrop again with different colour flowers? So work out the next step of attaching!

So now you have your curtain style & foliage design, get putting it all together, this is a must before the booing date!! Leaving it last minute is not a good idea, you need to be confident in putting it all together and knowing it is secure!

Pinterest is a good place to research backdrops, the styles are amazing!!!! Let it inspire you, put your own spin on things and get really creative! Go over the top if you want giving something new!!!!

3.1

You can purchase a number of stands for backdrops or make your own!! So for a more easy portable ones, you can purchase a number of them that unscrew to come apart, they are more metal poles and stands which can extend to 10ft both ways!

Or you can get a wooden base, you can make these yourself using timber, just make them sturdy give them a base, I made one and cemented them into plant pots, metal ones! To keep them sturdy from falling.

Another is arches, they have lots of styles in these and in different budgets, have a little research see what you like, a little tip, if you wanted to just try out an arch style, purchase a cheap arch and practice decorating it, getting the practice!

You can buy a range of flower wall panels if you're looking for that style which also have some in the grass and foliage style, these are connected by clipping into each panel, when I have done them before I have then cable tied them to the backdrop poles, which really secures them!

Do invest in at least one backdrop pole as these will also benefit, you will use it time and time again, they are especially good for doing demos!

Task – research into a backdrop stand suitable for you, remember how it will be transportable, put together, taken apart, a fixed one, or an arch, invest in your choice!!

4.1

Giving you a little more detail into the decorating of backdrops, so let's also touch on children's backdrops, these can be a little different, what can you use to decorate a children's backdrop??

Vinyl backdrops are really good which can be added with props made by yourself, and set the scene with extra additions, so here is my example Moana, was my little girl's favourite at the time!!!

So what did I do, I used a Moana vinyl backdrop, which had some characters on and the background was the sea & sand, I clipped it to my poles, which gave a background, I then attached bright coloured fans around the sides, giving colour and an extra touch. Then bringing the backdrop to life and creating a scene was fun, I used white wooden crates as a seating area, which I covered in a gold type net, I then painted coconuts with different designs to match the characters, I had a 5ft Moana and a 2ft cardboard cut-out & finished it with a floral number 2 in the same colours as the backdrop, a party bag & a balloon! The finishing look was just amazing, and it was a lot to do with the props!

So what else can you use props for???? Literally any backdrop, although don't overdo all of them, even sometimes just a lanterns or some tea lights can be a prop, twigs there are many little extras you can add!

I have also attached props to curtain nets before, it was a princess theme, I attached a cardboard cut-out shoe, crown & a castle, gave a great finish!

So many ways to decorate which doesn't even need to be the backdrop in itself think about the entire area!

Notes:

Module 9: the admin side

Objectives

- Types of administration roles you will need to do
- Essential paperwork
- Contracts
- Logos & business information

Introduction:

So with all businesses small or large administration tasks come into play! From emails to telephone calls and invoices, we need to keep on top of all our administration tasks.

When it comes to your paperwork does it all match? Look consistent? Professional? Would it sell your product? Do you have all the administration paperwork you need?

This is the first point of call for some customers in terms of communication, maybe they seen your social media or word of mouth, so they email you, your response is that first point of contact! Do you have a template set up on your email? Or have set up an automated response on your FB? This is an important part, you can set a little message that just informs the client, you are aware they have messaged and you will attend to them as soon as possible!

So let's look into all the types of administration roles you will do in the wedding style industry!

1.1 2.1

The most important and regular types of admin you will is, emails, quotes, invoices, contracts, mood boards, advertising & goal setting, I have put it all down as admin, as this moment in time it could be just yourself, working on the business, so it will all come under one roof for you!

Emails will be you're every day to day and answering messages on your social media platforms, sometimes this can take up a lot of your time, but it is one of the most important admin roles to stay on top of. Always keep an eye on your inbox, be aware if you have said you will get back to someone then you will, make notes if need to.

Quotes, on booking these will be something again you put together a lot, now you can design your own templates to start with or go straight in and sign up with an online company, prices for the software can vary, but worth a research if you want to save time, and have some money to put into your business! When I say design your own, use your logo and keep it consistent across all fields of paperwork!

Invoices, so your client has agreed to your quote so you are sending an invoice, now I sometimes send an invoice straight away, so I can minimise paperwork too, again use your logo and match all your paperwork! Your invoice is more about payment, items hired, when, and deposits & how to pay ect, make sure you include all the information you need your client to now!

Contracts, these are important, I will be honest it wasn't something I really worried about to start with luckily I never had a reason too, but as I have got more business, more knowledge and heard more stories, this is really important, get those contracts drawn up and signed, you and your client must know from day one what is involved in you both working together!

Other administration tasks such as mood boards, advertising & goal setting, are important to do for yourself and your business! Mood boards is good to do as mentioned before, they really help know the trends! Advertising is a must!!! This can be done in a number of ways, research the ways you want to do this and put time aside, this can take up time to start with but worth in the long run, then just set aside some goals weekly to keep on top of getting visible! Goals are so important for self-development and your business, it also helps keep you on track of what you're doing! Setting weekly and daily tasks can stop you side tracking, if you are anything like me, you get an idea and side track from what you was doing! So now I make sure I have my monthly goals, weekly and daily, try it once you will never look back!!

3.1

Contracts... So I touched on this earlier just how important they are!!! You really need to make sure on booking you get them contracts signed and sealed! I had my contract written up by a solicitor, I paid a small fee, and have them on my website under terms & conditions so they are always visible, but this is not something that is a must, I just like to have it! Then I send it out before booking, making sure they are signed and sent back, it really just covers you both!

Damage on items, money, items agreed on, items returned and set up information! Browse for some examples you can see mine on my website, or go straight to a solicitor explain what you do and what you want, let them do it all for you!

Task – very important to do this part, get your contract sorted and written up!

4.1

Logos so do you have a logo already? Drafting one? Or didn't really think you needed it??

Well you definitely should have one, this can be changed as and when, even if you steer in a different direction, you can change them! I think they are important as it is your symbol, this can go everywhere on all your social media platforms and paperwork, it will keep people remembering, your logo is linked to you!

So either get designing or get sharing!

Touching on some business information what do I mean by this, well there is a few other business things to do, that is worth looking into, sales funnels, a blog or a newsletter, you can build a list or client base, doing any of these, it gets people wanting to see more, signing up to see your offers and new products available!

Task – Which one will you do? Or will you do all 3???? Strat working on your lists!!

Notes:

Module 10: After set up & reviews

Objectives

- Final communication with your client
- Final communication with the venue
- Importance of reviews

Introduction:

So it is all finished, you done an amazing job!! Well done!!! It can be hard work & stressful, but the finishing piece is so worth it!! Take that time to really step back and just admire the work you did!!

Try and get as many pictures as possible, different angles, close ups and full room shots, sometimes you can end up rushing and not capture that hard work with pictures! Get good quality remember your backgrounds, crop take your time, once you leave you can't get them back, unless you contact the photographer, some are really good and supply, others like to keep for their portfolio only, so it is important to try and capture your own!

1.1

So you finished the event, your satisfied, the room looks amazing or whatever hard work you did!! The last part is sending that email, this is what I can put 'Hi ………. Just to let you know everything is set up, all went to plan and it looks amazing!! Congratulations again and enjoy every part of your

special day!! Glad you made us part of it'!! Or another one if I had to change something 'Hi ………..
Just to let you know everything is set, I did have to change around some tables, so the cake could fit into eye sight, it is beautiful and we didn't want to hide it away, hope you were happy with it! Then finish with the congratulations' Just then you have informed them, and they can read it and come back to you when they have a moment! It is more a curtesy email and it is lovely for your client to see that!

An advantage of this, is seals the event, gives it a finish, so they can be truly grateful for everything you done, and spread that gratefulness around to all their friends & family!

2.1

So this will mostly likely be when you collect all of your items, it is always good to ask for the coordinator if they are not available, just pass on a card to a member of staff! Especially if you're set up was talked about and liked, I was at a venue recently, the interior was like an old manor house, and the theme was hessian, the transformation was pretty amazing, it was praised by all the staff, and the management was brought in to have a look, so it was my chance to drop my details in! So it is good to try and get to see someone to finish your working experience of at any venue!

This can build up some links between you and the venue, which could lead into being put on the suppliers list! So remember to keep this in mind!

3.1

Once you have finished working with both your client and venue, why not ask for a review, build up them star ratings!

You could do this when you're sending those final emails or meeting with the coordinator on collection, explain in your email, if you were happy with our work and our communication throughout please leave us a review! Some do and sometimes it maybe they don't have the time too, so try not to be pushy although it can be frustrating, as it can take 5 minutes and it looks more professional to other potential customers, some people just don't see it as an important job to do!

As long as we have some reviews on our social media platform, it is something to work on!

The main purpose, is potential clients want to see your trusting, reliable, provide what you have agreed and if they can see other people saying all this, it gives the confidence they need to purchase and hire you!

So the task is if you have already done any events or even sold a product relating to your business, try and get them reviews in for it!!

If not remember this is an important task to do after!!

Notes:

Thank you for purchasing and reading! I hope this helps you to get your wedding & event styling business up and running, with the tips needed!

Would love to hear your feedback and your success!! So do keep in touch!
sarah@sparklingeventhire.com

At the moment I am writing and putting together a short practical course in backdrops, which will give people my inside big tip on how to create the ultimate backdrop, not once but continuously using the same nets/curtains!!!

To keep up with our latest courses, work, tips & general updates follow our social media platforms, Facebook, Instagram & Pinterest Sparkling Event Hire!

Thank you again

Sarah xxx

Printed in Great Britain
by Amazon